Fair Share

by Hollie J. Endres

Consultant: Brad Laager, MA, Math Educator
Little Falls Community Middle School

Yellow Umbrella Books
for early readers

Yellow Umbrella Books are published by Red Brick Learning
7825 Telegraph Road, Bloomington, Minnesota 55438
http://www.redbricklearning.com

Editorial Director: Mary Lindeen
Senior Editor: Hollie J. Endres
Senior Designer: Gene Bentdahl
Photo Researcher: Signature Design
Developer: Raindrop Publishing
Consultant: Brad Laager, MA, Math Educator, Little Falls Community Middle School
Conversion Assistants: Jenny Marks, Laura Manthe

Library of Congress Cataloging-in-Publication Data
Endres, Hollie J.
  Fair Share / by Hollie J. Endres
      p. cm.
  ISBN 0-7368-5852-0 (hardcover)
  ISBN 0-7368-5282-4 (softcover)
  1. Division—Juvenile literature. 2. Sharing—Juvenile literature. I. Title.
  QA115.E559 2005
  513.2'14—dc22
                                              2005016157

Photo Credits:
Cover: BananaStock Photos; Title Page: Brand X Pictures; Page 2: Eyewire/PhotoDisc Images;
Page 3: BananaStock Photos; Page 4: PhotoAlto; Page 5: Signature Design; Page 6: Digital Vision
Photos; Page 7: Signature Design; Page 8: Brand X Pictures; Page 9: Signature Design; Page 10:
BananaStock Photos; Page 11: Signature Design; Page 12: BananaStock Photos;
Page 13: Corbis; Page 14: Signature Design; Page 15: Brand X Pictures

1 2 3 4 5 6 11 10 09 08 07 06

Table of Contents

What Is Fair Sharing?

These students are learning about sharing. When you **share** with your friends, are you being **fair**? Sharing is fair if everyone gets the same amount.

How do we share fairly? We divide things evenly. Let's take a look at ways to share fairly.

Sharing for Two

Here are two friends. There are six cars to play with. How can they share fairly?

In order to be fair, each friend needs to have the same number of cars. If they take turns and pick one at a time, each will have three cars.

Is It Fair for Three?

These children are making lunch. There are three children helping. They are making six sandwiches. What would be fair for three?

They take turns and pick one sandwich at a time. How many will each child get? That's right! Each child will get two sandwiches.

Count It Out!

These four friends want to give their teacher flowers. They want to give her 12 flowers, or one dozen. How many should each friend pick to be fair? Let's count it out!

1, 2, 3, 4–now each friend has one flower. Then 5, 6, 7, and 8 makes two flowers for each. Next come 9, 10, 11, and 12. Now each friend has three flowers, and all is fair.

Can You Guess?

Here are five friends playing in the park. They have water to share. There are ten bottles of water for five friends. Can you guess what's fair?

Just as before, try counting it out:

1, 2, 3, 4, 5–

6, 7, 8, 9, 10.

How many does that make?

Each friend has two bottles of water!

Not Quite Enough

Sometimes when we share fairly, there are things left over. If there are three people and only two swings left, would that be fair? Why not?

12

Unequal numbers can sometimes be shared evenly. There are two friends, but only one apple. If they cut the apple in half, there will be two pieces. Is this fair?

You and your three friends are hungry.
There are five cookies. What can you do?

There is no way to share five cookies between four friends equally. You have a great idea. Now your little brother is happy, too!

Glossary

divide—to split something up

evenly—to have the same number or to be the same

fair—equal or even

share—to let someone else have part of something you have

unequal—not the same

Index

Word Count: 332
Early-Intervention Level: J